**DATE DUE**

|  |  |  |  |
|---|---|---|---|
|  |  |  |  |
|  |  |  |  |
|  |  |  |  |
|  |  |  |  |
|  |  |  |  |
|  |  |  |  |
|  |  |  |  |
|  |  |  |  |
|  |  |  |  |
|  |  |  |  |
|  |  |  |  |
|  |  |  |  |

# Red

## Moira Anderson

Heinemann Library
Chicago, Illinois

© 2006 Heinemann Library
a division of Reed Elsevier Inc.
Chicago, Illinois

Customer Service  888-454-2279
Visit our website at www.heinemannlibrary.com

Editorial: Moira Anderson, Carmel Heron
Page layout: Marta White, Heinemann Library Australia
Photo research: Jes Senbergs, Wendy Duncan
Production: Tracey Jarrett
Printed and bound in China by South China Printing Company Ltd.

09 08 07 06
10 9 8 7 6 5 4 3 2 1

**Library of Congress Cataloging-in-Publication Data**
Anderson, Moira (Moira Wilshin)
 Red / Moira Anderson.
      p. cm. -- (Finding colors)
 Includes index.
  ISBN 1-4034-7446-X (lib. bdg. : alk. paper) -- ISBN 1-4034-7451-6 (pbk. : alk. paper)
 1. Red--Juvenile literature. 2. Colors--Juvenile literature.  I. Title.
II. Series: Anderson, Moira  (Moira Wilshin).  Finding colors.
  QC495.5.A537 2005
  535.6--dc22

                                          2005009724

**Acknowledgments**
The author and publisher are grateful to the following for permission to reproduce copyright
material: Rob Cruse Photography: p. **10**; Corbis: pp. **8, 20, 21, 23** (cotton, celebrate); Getty
Images: p. **15**; Getty Images/PhotoDisc: pp. **22, 24**; PhotoDisc: pp. **4, 5** (all items), **6, 7, 9,
11, 12, 13, 14, 16, 17, 19, 23** (skin, stem, wool, berries, leaves); photolibrary.com: p. **18**.

Front cover photograph permission of Tudor Photography, back cover photographs permission
of photolibrary.com (ladybug) and PhotoDisc (pepper).

Every effort has been made to contact copyright holders of any material reproduced in this book.
Any omissions will be rectified in subsequent printings if notice is given to the publisher.

Many thanks to the teachers, library media specialists, reading instructors, and educational
consultants who have helped develop the Read and Learn/Lee y aprende brand.

# Contents

What Is Red? . . . . . . . . . . . . . . . . . . . . . .4

What Red Things Can I Eat? . . . . . . . . .6

What Red Clothes Can I Wear? . . . . . . .8

What Is Red on Buildings? . . . . . . . . . . .10

What Is Red at Home? . . . . . . . . . . . . . .12

Can I Find Red Things in a City? . . . . .14

Can I Find Red Things in a Forest? . . .16

Are There Red Animals? . . . . . . . . . . . . .18

How Do People Celebrate with Red? . .20

Quiz . . . . . . . . . . . . . . . . . . . . . . . . . . . .22

Glossary . . . . . . . . . . . . . . . . . . . . . . . . .23

Index . . . . . . . . . . . . . . . . . . . . . . . . . . .24

Some words are shown in bold, **like this**.
You can find them in the glossary on page 23.

# What Is Red?

Red is a color.

What different colors can you see in this picture?

The color red is all around.

What do you do with these
red things?

# What Red Things Can I Eat?

Strawberries are good to eat.

When they are red, we can pick and eat them.

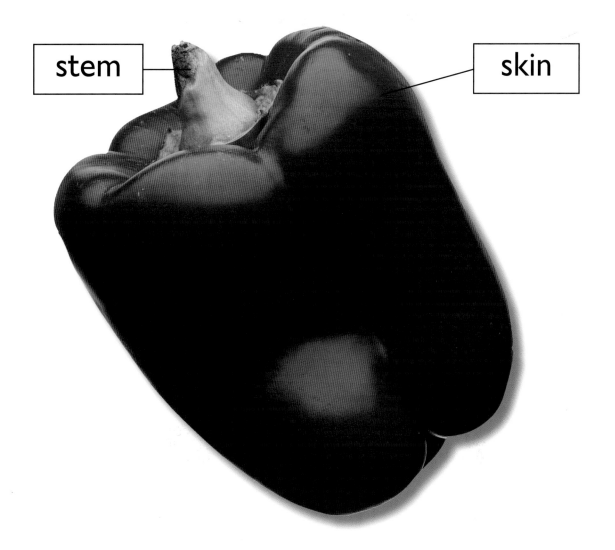

stem

skin

Some peppers are red.

They have red **skin** and a green **stem**.

# What Red Clothes Can I Wear?

This shirt is made of red **cotton**.

Cotton keeps you cool.

These red mittens are made of **wool**.

Wool keeps your hands warm.

# What Is Red on Buildings?

Some buildings are made
of red bricks.

Bricks are hard and strong.

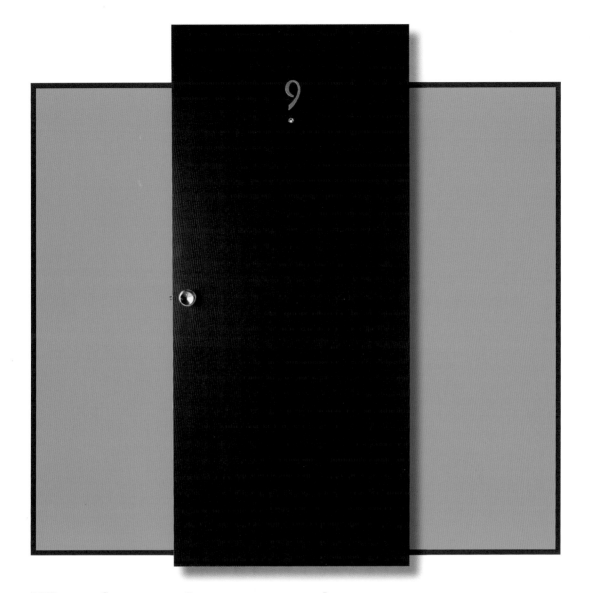

This front door is red.

It is made of wood and painted red.

# What Is Red at Home?

handle grips

seat

This tricycle is red.

It has a red seat and handle grips.

This mug is red.

It keeps the cocoa hot.

# Can I Find Red Things in a City?

These traffic lights are sometimes red.

When the light is red, traffic must stop.

This fire truck is red.

It is used to fight fires.

# Can I Find Red Things in a Forest?

Red **berries** grow in a forest.

They are easy to see in the snow.

The **leaves** of this tree are red.

Some leaves turn red in the fall.

# Are There Red Animals?

Red animals live in gardens.

Ladybugs are red insects.

Red animals live in the sea.

This starfish is red and yellow.

# How Do People Celebrate with Red?

People **celebrate** Chinese New Year with lots of red.

They put up red lanterns.

People celebrate with fireworks.

Red fireworks look good in the night sky.

# Quiz

What red things can you see?

Look for the answers on page 24.

# Glossary

**berry**
small, round, juicy fruit

**celebrate**
do something special to show a day
or event is important

**cotton**
material made from the cotton plant;
used to make clothes

**leaf**
flat part of a plant that grows from
the stem or a branch

**skin**
outer layer of vegetables or fruit

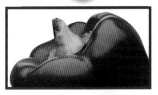

**stem**
center part of a plant

**wool**
thread made from soft hair of sheep;
used to make clothes

# Index

animals  18, 19

berries  16, 23

bricks  10

door  11

fire truck  15

fireworks  21

ladybugs  18

lanterns  20

leaves  17, 23

mittens  9

mug  13

pepper  7

shirt  8

starfish  19

strawberries  6

traffic lights  14

tricycle  12

Answers to the quiz on page 22

paint

smock

table

chairs

## Notes to parents and teachers

Reading non-fiction texts for information is an important part of a child's literacy development. Readers can be encouraged to ask simple questions and then use the text to find the answers. Each chapter in this book begins with a question. Read the questions together. Look at the pictures. Talk about what the answer might be. Then read the text to find out if your predictions were correct. To develop readers' enquiry skills, encourage them to think of other questions they might ask about the topic. Discuss where you could find the answers. Assist children in using the contents page, picture glossary and index to practise research skills and new vocabulary.